T0094588

LITTLE DOGS: NEW AND SELECTED

Also by Michael Crummey

LITTLE
DOGS
NEW AND
SELECTED

MICHAEL
CRUMMEY

ANANSI

Copyright © 2016 Michael Crummey

Published in Canada in 2016 and in the USA in 2016 by House of Anansi Press Inc.

www.houseofanansi.com

All rights reserved. No part of this publication may be reproduced or transmitted in any form or by any means, electronic or mechanical, including photocopying, recording, or any information storage and retrieval system, without permission in writing from the publisher.

House of Anansi Press is committed to protecting our natural environment. As part of our efforts, the interior of this book is printed on paper made from second-growth forests and is acid-free.

21 20 19 18 17   2 3 4 5 6

Library and Archives Canada Cataloguing in Publication

Crummey, Michael
[Poems. Selections]
Little dogs : new and selected poems / Michael Crummey.

Issued in print and electronic formats.
ISBN 978-1-4870-0097-4 (bound).—ISBN 978-1-4870-0098-1 (pdf)
—ISBN 978-1-4870-0096-7 (pbk.)

I. Title. II. Title: Poems. Selections.

PS8555.R84A6 2016   C811'.54   C2015-907211-5
                                             C2015-907212-3

Library of Congress Control Number: 2015955234

Book design: Alysia Shewchuk
Typesetting: Marijke Friesen

We acknowledge for their financial support of our publishing program the Canada Council for the Arts, the Ontario Arts Council, and the Government of Canada through the Canada Book Fund.

Printed and bound in Canada

MIX
Paper from
responsible sources
FSC
www.fsc.org   FSC® C004071

Born fifty years ago to raise my voice this high, and no higher.
—Leonard Cohen

ARGUMENTS WITH GRAVITY 1996

HARD LIGHT 1998

NEW POEMS

LITTLE DOGS: NEW AND SELECTED

ARGUMENTS
WITH
GRAVITY
1996

MORNING   LABRADOR COAST

Morning   Labrador coast
my father is thirteen
no, younger still
eleven maybe twelve
shivering to warm himself in the dark

The rustle of surf behind him
the passiveness of it at this hour
the grumble of men waking early
in the shacks
the steady muffle of piss
smacking a low mound of moss at his feet

He's almost given up on childhood
works a full share on the crew
smokes dried rock-moss rolled in
brown paper out of sight of his father

Each morning he makes fists to work the stiffness
out of his hands and wrists
the skin cracked by sea salt
the joints swollen by sleep after hours of work
he soaks them in the warm salve
of his urine
shakes them dry in the cold air
and turning back to the shacks
he sees stars disappearing in the blue
first light breaking out over the water
the dories overturned on the grey beach
waiting

COD (1)

Some days the nets came up so full
there was enough cod to swamp the boat
and part of the catch came in with other crews
once they'd filled their own trapskiff to the gunwales,
the silver-grey bodies of the fish rippling
like the surface of a lake
the weight of them around their legs
like stepping thigh-deep into water

Most of the work was splitting and curing—
the thin gutting knife slivered up the belly
and everything pulled clear with the sound bone,
liver into the oil barrel
the thick tongue cut from the throat
and the splayed fish ready for salting then
set out on a flake to dry

This until one in the morning sometimes
a river of cod across the cutting table
in the yellow swirl of kerosene lamps
and everyone up by three or four
to get back out to the nets with the light

There was no talk of sleep when
the cod were running strong,
a few good weeks could make a season—
if they dreamt at all
in those three brief hours a night
they dreamt of the fish
the cold sweet weight of them,
fin and tail flickering in their heads
like light on the water

The day my grandfather died he ate
a meal of salt beef and cabbage in his
sick bed, his appetite returning for
the first time in weeks, the skin
hanging from the bones of his face
like an oversized suit.

My father had gone in to see him
before church that morning, fifteen years old
and thinking the old man was recovering;
they spoke for a few minutes about the cold
and about going out in the spring,
and then my grandfather asked his son for
a cigarette.

Summers, after the capelin had rolled,
the cod moved into water too deep for the traps
and the two of them would spend the days jigging,
standing at the gunnel with a line down
ten fathoms, repeating the rhythmic full-arm jig
as if they were unsuccessfully trying to
start an engine.

Mid-afternoon they'd stop to eat,
stoking the galley's firebox to stew cods' heads
and boil tea, then my grandfather would sit aft
with a pipe, pulling his oilskin jacket
over his head until he was finished.
He'd known for years that my father was smoking
on the sly though he'd never acknowledged it,

hid beneath a coat to give his son
a chance to sneak a cigarette
before they got back to work.

The air in the sick room was so cold
their breath hung in clouds between them.
My grandfather was about to die of cancer or TB
and his son sat beside the bed, his pockets
empty for once of Bugle or Target tobacco,
telling his father he had no cigarette to give him
which happened to be the truth, and felt like
a lie to them both.

COD (2)

August.
    My father has sent the crew
home early for the second year in a row
the cod so scarce he can do
the work himself and still have time
to sit in the evenings
time to think about the flour and molasses
the netting, the coils of rope and twine
the tea and sugar and salt he took
on credit in the spring.

Every night he dreams of them plentiful
the size of the fish years ago
big around as your thigh
the thick shiver of their bodies
coming up in the cod traps.

He turned seventeen this February past
his father has been dead two short seasons.
Alone at the water's edge he sits
mending a useless net and smoking
already two-hundred dollars in debt
to the merchants.

There are no cod in the whole frigging ocean.

LILACS

The well is contaminated and we have to
haul a bucket of water up from the brook;
we pull handfuls of lilacs from the trees
outside the open windows and set them
in glasses through the house to mask the smell
of rooms shut up with themselves for years

There are old saucers of poison
placed on countertops and mantlepieces, spoor in the pantry
and Dad tells me how he'd chase mice through
the house with a stick when he was a boy
although it was considered bad luck for the fishing
and his father forbid killing them
during the season;
                        in Labrador, he says
you could follow the paths they'd beaten
through the long grass in the dark
but no one raised a hand to them all summer

There are still two beds in the room
where my father was born in 1930
and we roll out our sleeping bags there
then walk to the corner store for food and beer;
later I watch his face in the pale light
of the Coleman lantern
try to connect him to what I know of that time
dust bowl photographs, soup kitchens
stories of vagrants at back doors offering
to chop wood for a meal
but I know I have it hopelessly wrong—

he wanted nothing more for me
than that I should grow up a stranger to all this
that his be one of the lives I have not lived

        After the lights are put out
there is a silence broken only by the sounds
we make as we shift in our beds and
the occasional scuffle of mice in the hallway;
the age of the house gives a musty
undertone to the sweet smell of the lilacs
and it seems stronger in the darkness
so that I imagine I am breathing in what's left
of the world my father knew
while the part of him that has never
managed to leave here is asleep across the room

FORGE

Hefei, Anhui Province, China

Halfway to the school there's a group
of blacksmiths working at small portable forges
along the roadside, hammering iron bodies
around the words in their mouths,
a coal shovel almost there on the anvil,
two men struggling with its red-hot syllable
like stubborn lexicographers,
their alternating hammer strokes
demanding *what do you mean?*
what do you mean goddamn it?
while the sun beats across their backs

A toddler wearing crotchless pants
stops to piss in the street nearby
and there's something disarmingly true
about his simple squat in the middle
of bicycle traffic,
his head shaved bald as a Buddhist monk's,
the unconcerned look of meditation
on his face as he urinates
        and I can't help connecting the two
in this afternoon heat,
the boy finishing up now and straightening
as if from prayer,
the smiths behind him slamming
their metal tongues against
unrepentant shapelessness,
parts of a whole the poem includes,
is included in, but I can't quite get it,

squinting against the difficult sunlight,
and no one else seems to notice a thing—

young Buddha wanders off in search of a parent,
the two men break for a cigarette and some conversation
and maybe there was nothing there
at all—

RIVERS/ROADS

I thought I was following a track of freedom
and for awhile it was
   —Adrienne Rich

Consider the earnestness of pavement
its dark elegant sheen after rain
its insistence on leading you somewhere

A highway wants to own the landscape
it sections prairie into neat squares
swallows mile after mile of countryside
to connect the dots of cities and towns
to make sense of things

A river is less opinionated
less predictable
it doesn't argue with gravity
its history is a series of delicate negotiations with
geography and time

Wet your feet all you want
Hericlitus says
it's never the river you remember

A road repeats itself incessantly
obsessed with its own small truth
it wants you to believe in something particular

The destination you have in mind when you set out
is nowhere you have ever been

Where you arrive finally depends on
how you get there
by river or by road

HARD
LIGHT
1998

WHAT'S LOST

The Labrador coastline is a spill of islands,
salt-shaker tumble of stone,
a cartographer's nightmare—
on the coastal boat fifty years ago
the third mate marked his location after dark
by the outline of a headland against the stars,
the sweetly acrid smell of bakeapples blowing off
a stretch of bog to port or starboard,
navigating without map or compass
where hidden shoals shadow the islands
like the noise of hammers echoed across a valley.

The largest are home to harbours and coves,
a fringe of clapboard houses
threaded by dirt road,
grey-fenced cemeteries sinking
unevenly into mossy grass.
Even those too small to be found on the map
once carried a name in someone's mind,
a splinter of local history—
a boat wracked up in a gale of wind,
the roof-wrecked remains of a stagehouse
hunkered in the lee.

Most of what I want him to remember
lies among those islands, among the maze
of granite rippling north a thousand miles,
and what he remembers is all I have a claim to.
My father nods toward the coastline,
to the bald stone shoals almost as old as light—

That was fifty years ago, he says,
as a warning, wanting me to understand
that what's forgotten is lost
and most of this he cannot even recall
forgetting

STEALING BAIT

Nain, 1957

The year he came to teach at the school
someone began following the trappers' lines
through the bush, stealing bait,
setting free whatever was found alive.
There was talk of spirits and such at first,
we should have known it was just the white man.
He'd come into the classroom with bandaged hands
or a nip in his face where the foxes got at him
when he knelt to pry them loose.

An elder went down to see him,
explained how the legs in the trap
are broken, the freed animals
limping off to die of starvation
in a hole somewhere, it made no difference.

He was a crazy sonofabitch anyway,
off in the woods all alone like that,
talking to the trees. It was no surprise
he killed himself that winter,
a rifle pushed up under his chin.
He had taken off one shoe to fire the round,
his big toe shoved into the snare
of the trigger guard, the bone
broken clean by the barrel's kick.

What you'd imagine the sound of
an orchestra tuning up might look like,
cacophony of silver and black at your feet.
Spawning capelin in their numberless legions
washed onto grey sand beaches
like survivors of a shipwreck,
their teeming panic reduced to helpless
writhing while boys scoop them up
with buckets, with dipnets.
They migrate a thousand nautical miles
for this, each wave rolling to shore
like another bus stuffed with
passengers bound for oblivion,
limbs and heads hanging recklessly
through the open windows.

Most of them rotted above the landwash
or found their way onto gardens
planted with potatoes in those days,
except for the few we laid out
to dry beside the shed,
neat rows of the tiny fish
endlessly buzzed over by houseflies
like crazy eighth notes on a staff.
Roasted them above open flame
until they were black and they tasted
much as you'd imagine burnt fish would
but we ate them regardless
head and tail together.
They had come such a long way

and given themselves up so completely
and in such an awful silence
that we felt obliged to
acquire the taste.

There was one in every fishing crew of four or five, brought along to cook and keep the shack in decent shape, and do their part with making the fish when the traps were coming up full, cutting throats or keeping the puncheon tub filled with water. They helped set the salt cod on the bawns for drying in August, called out of the kitchen if a squall of rain came on to gather it up before it was ruined.

Most were girls whose families needed the wage, some as young as thirteen, up before sunrise to light the fire for tea and last to bed at night, the hot coals doused with a kettle of water.

Usually the girl had her own room beside the skipper's downstairs, the rest of the crew shoved into bunks under the attic eaves on mattresses stuffed with wood shavings. Sometimes it was only a blanket hung from the rafters that stood between her and the men.

When the work slowed after the capelin scull, a fiddle might be coaxed from a corner on Saturday nights, lips set to a crock of moonshine, followed by a bit of dancing, heels hammering the planks down in the bunkhouse. The single boys courted hard, they'd fall in love just to make it easier getting through the season. There was a carousel of compliments, of flirting, there were comments about the light in a girl's eyes or the darkness of her hair. There was romance of a sort to be considered: coals to be fanned alive or soused with the wet of a cold shoulder. The fire of loneliness and fatigue smouldering in the belly.

Most of it came to nothing but idle talk and foolishness, though every year there were marriages seeded on the Labrador islands, along with a few unhappier things. A child sailing home pregnant in the fall and four men swearing they never laid a hand upon her.

Sent to the ice after white coats,
rough outfit slung on coiled rope belts,
they stooped to the slaughter: gaffed pups,
slit them free of their spotless pelts.

The storm came on unexpected.
Stripped clean of bearings, the watch struck
for the waiting ship and missed it.
Hovelled in darkness two nights then,

bent blindly to the sleet's raw work,
bodies muffled close for shelter,
stepping in circles like blinkered mules.
The wind jerking like a halter.

Minds turned by the cold, lured by small
comforts their stubborn hearts rehearsed,
men walked off ice floes to the arms
of phantom children, wives; of fires

laid in imaginary hearths.
Some surrendered movement and fell,
moulting warmth flensed from their faces
as the night and bitter wind doled out

their final, pitiful wages.

'AND NOW TO MAKE A START AS A BOY OF VERY LITTLE UNDERSTANDING.' (1876)

After a single season jigging cod
I gave up on the ocean,
boarded a steamship bound
for Little Bay Mines where
I secured a position
picking for copper;
kept at it through the winter,
a long shadow working
effortlessly beside me
while my back was shaken crooked
by the jabber of pickhead on rock,
my hands too numb
at the end of a shift
to properly hold a spoon

In June I jacked up and went
back to fishing, shipping out
with a crew headed to the French Shore,
happy just to be on the water
after seven months discovering darkness
in the mine

Salt air like a handful of brine
held to the face of an unconscious man
coming slowly to his senses

Now as the sails are set a sailor must know
all the ropes or running gear before he can
reef, clew or furl, and the names of the ropes
are as follows. Jib halliards. Troat halliards.
Peak, Royal and Topgallant halliards.
Royal braces, Topgallant braces, Topsail braces.
Fore and Main braces. Preventer main braces.
After main braces. Sheets and lifts for the
Topgallant, Topsail and Main. Clewgarnets.
Foretack, Topsail buntlines, Reef burtons.
Leech lines. Slab lines. Spanker's brail and
outhall. Boom topping outhall. Flying jib
downhall, jib downhall, fore topmast stays.
Which is not to mention the standing rigging
on which the sailors move among the ropes
in all weather and sometimes appear
to be spiders mending a web, while at others
they appear to be caught and helpless as flies
in a web of someone else's design.

'ARRIVED IN HONG KONG, NOVEMBER 9. THE HISTORIES OF CHINA' (1888)

Sailed into the harbour early morning
and made our ship fast to the old stone quay,
the Chinese coming down in hundreds to greet us—
a queer lot at first glance, I guess,
the men wearing braided pigtails
and the women stepping as if
they were walking on glass,
their stunted feet bound tight as reefed sails

Went ashore after tea and received some peculiar looks
though I was turned out as well as a sailor can manage;
stopped into a bar where I checked myself
in the glass and found no fault to speak of,
perhaps it was my ears
they were staring at

Dusk when I found my way back to the waterfront
and three parts drunk by then,
14000 miles from Newfoundland
to the east and west
and can get no further from my home if I wanted—
2000 years before the birth of Christ
the Emperor Yu divided this empire
into nine provinces and etched
their borders on nine copper vessels . . .

The stars came out over the Pacific then
and they came out over me,
only twenty-six years old and all the histories
of China at my back

Desert the colour of winter sunlight,
a yellow that is almost white, shadowless,
constant shift of sand like
a tide swell beneath your feet.
Hills on the horizon as red as blood.

The Commandments carried down Mount Sinai
by Moses in sandals, his feet blistered
by the heat of God's presence,
lettered stone scorched by the sun,
his bare hands burning.

All of this was once under water—
mountains rose from the parting flood
like the Israelites
marching out of the Red Sea
to walk parched into wilderness,
sucking moisture from handfuls
of hoarfrost.

I have spent my life on the ocean,
seven years now I have worked
on the high seas,
my hands blistered by the water's salt,
my tongue thick and dry as leather.
The desert was familiar to me,
I knew something of what it
demands of a person,
what it can teach.

I understood it is mostly thirst
that makes a place holy.

In seven years sailing I laid eyes
on the rocks of Newfoundland but twice,
skirting Cape Race shoals for Halifax
and again on the way to Boston,
looking away as quick as that
on both occasions;
I could hear her singing across the water
and stopped up my ears,
I suppose I knew I'd never be able
to leave a second time

Intending a brief visit to family last fall
I married a woman in Tomwalls Harbour,
paying the old priest three dollars
to splice us; she held me like a tree
grown through a wire fence
and I could not get away in the spring
though I said that was what I wanted

Bought a sloop and started trading
wood and coal and dry goods
around the Bay of Exploits,
gave up the sea for memories
bound as I was to the island of my birth;
I wanted an excuse to stay and found one
but a man's heart is never satisfied
and there is still a song
in my head on times that
will not let me be

'BOAT BUILDING.' (1899)

Before the snow settles in
have your wood cut and
carried to the dockyard where
you can work away at her
through the winter.

Scarf the joints to frame her out,
fit the beams, sides and stanchions,
then caulk her timber tight with
old rags or moss chinked in
with maul and chisel.
Give her a name before you
fit her out with rigging,
christen her bow with a prayer.
When the spring drives off the ice
launch her into the harbour
and hope for the best
when you let her go.

Remember this if you can:
a boat on the water belongs
to the water first
regardless of her name
or who it is that names her.

He sat reading a paper until eleven,
knocked out his pipe,
doused the lamp.
His wife already in bed
he undressed in the darkness,
folding his clothes across
a chairback.
Around midnight he turned out
to get his knife,
his wife sitting up to see
what he was about.

He had two daughters,
the eldest screamed *Daddy Daddy*
look what you have done
and he ran out the door
to the canal where he drowned himself.
I watched them haul his body
from the water and carry him
to the dead house.

He was a stranger to me—
met him coming across from Tilt Cove
aboard the *Marion* two days before.
I slept next to him in the forecastle
and he did not stir through the night.

When he bolted from the house
he carried the knife with him
and there's no saying
where he left it.
In the mouth of the harbour maybe,
the silver blade still catching light
beneath the shallow water.

I am an old man now
hard aground in Twillingate
and telling tales to skeptics,
my finger dipped in tea
to sketch a map across the table.

The young ones drop by with
whiskey to hear me talk,
I give them streets
cobbled with marble in Italy,
the long spiralling line of China's wall,
the songs I learned while drinking
with the darkies in Virginia,
those sounds as old as a continent . . .
I can tell they don't buy
the half of it.

It's an old sailor's portion
to be disbelieved so often
that he begins to doubt himself;
the best part of my life has passed
as a shadow, and shadows are what
I am left with—
perhaps every place I have ever been
is imaginary, like the Equator
or the points on a compass.

Don't ask me what is real
when you hear me talk,
I can only tell you
what I remember.

Look down at the table.
The map has already disappeared.

A picture that was never taken, infrared photograph of the square wooden house in Western Bay, a record of heat and its loss. Most of the building sits in darkness, a shallow haze of escaping energy pink above the shingles, deeper and more insistent where the chimney rises into the night air.

Downstairs, the kitchen is a ball of flame, the draughty windows spilling fire. The wood stove at the centre, as dark as a heart, stoked full with junks of spruce and throwing heat like a small sun. The family sits as far back as kitchen walls allow, shirt sleeves rolled to the elbows, sweat on their brows, the temperature pushing eighty-five degrees.

In the next room, behind the closed kitchen door, a film of ice forms on water left sitting in a cup. Steam rises from the head of the woman who walks in from the kitchen to retrieve it and in the photograph her neat bun of hair is haloed by a shaggy orange glow.

Later, the outline of sleepers under blankets in the upstairs bedrooms mapped by a dull cocoon of warmth, a bright circle lying at their feet: beach rocks heated in the oven and carried to bed in knitted woolen covers. The outrageous autumn-red pulse fading as the house moves deeper into night, the incandescent warmth of it slowly guttering into darkness.

After Father died I got a crew together and went down the Labrador myself; I was just sixteen then and the arse gone out of the fishery besides, it only took me two seasons to wind up a couple of hundred dollars in the hole.

I landed the job at the mine intending to work off the debt and go back to the fishing right away. One of the other stationers on Breen's Island wrote to me once I'd been gone five or six years, asking after the boat and the stage, said they were rotting away as it was. I told him to use what he wanted and never heard any more about it. I knew by then it was all over for me anyway.

My first Christmas home from the mine I'd gone up to see old man Sellars; he had me in for a glass of whiskey and a slice of cake and talked about forgiving some of what I owed him, but I wouldn't hear of it. Pulled out a slender stack of fifties and counted off two hundred dollars into his hand. New bills, the paper crisp as the first layer of ice over a pond in the fall. Then I had another glass of whiskey and then I went home out of it, half drunk and feeling like I'd lost something for good.

I, Ellen Rose of Western Bay in the Dominion of
Newfoundland. Married woman, mother, stranger to my
grandchildren. In consideration of natural love and affection,
hereby give and make over unto my daughter Minnie Jane
Crummey of Western Bay, a meadow garden situated at
Riverhead, bounded to the north and east by Loveys Estate, to
the south by John Lynch's land, to the west by the local road
leading countrywards. Bounded above by the sky, by the blue
song of angels and God's stars. Below by the bones of those
who made me.

I leave nothing else. Every word I have spoken the wind
has taken, as it will take me. As it will take my grandchildren's
children, their heads full of fragments and my face not among
those. The day will come when we are not remembered, I
have wasted no part of my life in trying to make it otherwise.

In witness thereof I have set my hand and seal this
thirteenth day of December, One thousand Nine hundred and
Thirty Three.

Her
Ellen **X** Rose
Mark

Ingredients:
    1 quart of dandelion flowers picked from the meadow garden
    4 gallons of water carried up from the brook
    2 and one half pounds of sugar from the winter store
    1 teaspoon of cream of tartar, the rind and juice of 2 lemons

Boil the works in the beer pot for twenty minutes, turn it out
into a pan and let it cool. When the liquid is new-milk warm,
add four tablespoons of yeast and let it work for about a day,
until you can see the tiny bubbles start to rise. Boil your
bottles and siphon the beer from your pan, then cork tightly.
Keep them in a cool place or the bottles may burst, the small
explosions like rifle shots in the middle of the night, your
shoes sticking to the floor for weeks, the house stinking of
yeast and alcohol.

Fit to drink after two days in the bottle. A glassful will
straighten a crooked spine. Three bottles enough to put a song
in your heart and the heart of your neighbour come for a visit;
four enough to light the flicker of dandelion flames in your
sorry eyes. Five will set your head on fire, have your
neighbour dancing around the kitchen with a broom, singing
the only line he knows of *The Tennessee Waltz*. Send him
home with one less sock than he came with. Wake you early
with the tick of a cooling engine in your skull, your face the
colour of ash. Your neighbour's wife wondering what became
of that missing sock, and he will never find an explanation to
satisfy her.

Makes about 3 dozen.

I was twenty years younger than my husband, his first wife
dead in childbirth. I agreed to marry him because he was a
good fisherman, because he had his own house and he was
willing to take in my mother and father when the time came.
It was a practical decision and he wasn't expecting more than
that. Two people should never say the word love before they've
eaten a sack of flour together, he told me.

The night we married I hiked my nightdress around my
thighs and shut my eyes so tight I saw stars. Afterwards I
went outside and I was sick, throwing up over the fence. He
came out the door behind me and put his hand to the small
of my back. It happens your first time, he said. It'll get better.

I got pregnant right away and then he left for the
Labrador. I dug the garden, watched my belly swell like a seed
in water. Baked bread, bottled bakeapples for the winter store,
cut the meadow grass for hay. After a month alone I even
started to miss him a little.

The baby came early, a few weeks after my husband
arrived home in September. We had the minister up to the
house for the baptism the next day, Angus Maclean we named
him, and we buried him in the graveyard in the Burnt Woods
a week later. I remember he started crying at the table the
morning of the funeral and I held his face against my belly
until he stopped, his head in my hands about the size of the
child before it was born. I don't know why sharing a grief will
make you love someone.

I was pregnant again by November. I baked a loaf of
bread and brought it to the table, still steaming from the oven.
Set it on his plate whole and stood there looking at him.

That's the last of that bag of flour, I told him. And he smiled at me and didn't say anything for a minute. I'll pick up another today, he said finally.

And that's how we left it for a while.

Breen's Island lies in the mouth of Indian Tickle, two rocks hinged by a narrow strand of beach, fused vertebrae in a long spine of water running between two larger islands. He hasn't laid eyes on the place in fifty years and hoped to this afternoon, but there's a heavy sea on as they labour through Domino Run and the Skipper won't chance the passage. Rain, and grey waves breaking on the headlands, water worrying stone. He and his son stare down through the Tickle with binoculars as the ship staggers by the northern entrance, Breen's Island out of sight behind a crook of land.

As they trace the arm of the Tickle in open water, he names the pairs of islands to port: the Gannets, the Ferrets, the Wolves. The seascape like a book of rhymes from childhood he is unforgetting in fragments. He points out the stretch of bog where they picked bakeapples in August, the deep water shoals best for jigging cod at season's end. And Breen's Island just over the cliff to starboard, as good as fifty years away. When the ship clears the arm they turn to watch the Tickle recede, passing the binoculars back and forth between them. Half a dozen tiny islands in the mouth, one revealed behind the other like a series of Chinese boxes each hidden inside the last. *Do you see it*, his son asks, and he grins uncomfortably, as if he wants to say yes for his son's sake but can't. They aren't close enough to make it out for sure. He knows they never will be. The ship heaves south on the dark swell toward Red Point, Indian Tickle slowly blurring out of focus.

The steady drift of rain like a cataract clouding his eyes.

SALVAGE

2001

His body divorced him slowly
like a flock of birds leaving
a wire, one set of wings at a time—
still in sight, but past retrieving.

Extremities first, his right foot
dropping asleep, forcing a limp
until the left faltered numb,
conspiring to abort every step.

Fingers and tongue deadened, as if
wrapped in a muffle of feather down—
each affliction painless and shameful,
like a ship run aground in sand.

His infant child seemed to chase him,
her development a mirror
image of his progressive loss;
her wonder, reversed, his terror.

Still, he got on with things, wrote
the last poems, read. Tried to swallow
the panic that galled his throat,
never mentioned the dream of crows.

After his voice abandoned him
his wife scissored an alphabet
and they relearned the grace of words—
letters raised like a wick, and lit.

At the end he was stripped of all
but that fire, its sad, splendid
glow. When his wife offered him
the sedative they knew would end it

he asked "How long will I sleep?"
spelled it out, letter by letter.
The fear had left them both by then.
She told him, "Until you're better."

Heading for a cheap-beer-on-tap
greasy spoon at College and Bathurst
he passes a man with his hand out,
practised nonchalance, expecting nothing
to cheat disappointment.
The sky above them so faded
it's barely legible, a battalion
of yellow street lights feeding
on the tender shoots of constellations.

He's brought an old edition of
The New American Poets,
sips his way through two pints,
through Kerouac and Ginsberg,
their cities alive in those lines
like ugly flowers in a water glass
and both of them dead now,
Monday Night Football on
television above the bar—
brute force veined with strategies
so intricate the game looks
almost graceful from a distance,
the remote choreography of stars.

The book holding its hands
out to the air like the small
perfect leaves of a tree
feeding on sunlight.

Shower room's peace shattered by boys launched
like rockets, their racket sudden as rain
on a tin roof. Shyness sharp as a sprain
makes him wince at the sight of his paunch,

his penis crouched in its thicket of curls.
But the boys ignore the naked man beside
them, their voices pitched toward registers
beyond hearing, skin translucent white,

everything about them in ascendance,
inching toward their adult heights
without hesitation or reluctance.
They orbit his silence like satellites

trailing the dead weight of stars—
there's no way to warn them what lies ahead
and he's torn by a father's helpless regret,
seeing them so unguarded, so free of scars.

HOW HE CARRIED IT

It hovered in the boy's head pale
as a daylight moon

It lit him up like a field
under a hail of lightning,
it torched the buildings locked
and almost hidden under brush
in the unfenced backyard of his mind

It travelled in his blood like blooms
of silt stirred from a river bottom,
it ticked like a clock toward
some alarm his body
lay awake for,
it made him feel ancient and
unrecoverable and lonely
for his friends

It churned inside him
like the crankshaft of the planet,
darkness endlessly turning
toward a deeper darkness
he had no name for

It settled on him like squatters
claiming farmland lying fallow,
like summer dusk staining
the distant hills blue

She was uncharacteristically late
and they both fought a sense of wild
dread, the certainty of her condition
filling their heads like the feedback hum
of an amplifier overheating.
Nothing for it but surrender to fate—
they sat wringing their hands, debating
names for the inevitable child.

She was a year older and did him
the favour of feigning disbelief
when he confessed she was his first.
Two kids in love: he'd have proposed
and she'd have said yes, for better or worse,
if it hadn't ended with the sudden relief
of menstrual blood staining her clothes.

Years later it came to him second-hand,
she'd married and had a son,
that both nearly died during the birth:
the baby obstructed, a long delay
in utero starving him of oxygen.
It was chance that either survived
and the damage to the child's brain
meant he'd never manage to hold
a fork, or take an uncomplicated breath.

Heard nothing more till he was told
she lost her son at the age of five.
He didn't even know the boy's name.

THE KISS

He's almost given up on you, sleeper,
on the part of himself that imagines
nuzzling the fat pink erasers of your feet,
thinks of nursing bruises at your temples
where the forceps would have coaxed
the greedy flame of your voice into
his cupped and waiting hands.
His selfishness is the spell that holds you
submerged like a lost child in a fairy tale,
your absence ripening on the branches of
these words like orchard fruit,
and his mouth on his lover's body
so close to the place you would stir
startles him with nostalgia and loneliness,
like hearing the old stories in which
a beautiful sleeper is woken with a kiss.
He troubles you now like any father,
haunted by his failures, wanting
forgiveness for loving you only as well
as his weaknesses allowed, for turning
his back when he might have touched
his lips to your dreaming face,
watched your eyes startle open
on the brightly candled stage of your life.

Talk exhausted for the night
he walks her home in silence,
comes back to the small wreck
of the meal, empty containers, food scraps,
dishes stacked beside the sink
like beads on an abacus reckoning
an emotional failure's tired repetition.
Equations that map the stars turn
in and in on themselves like prayers
sieved and refined until symbol = value
but a life bogs down in simple arithmetic.
He's never known more than
what he doesn't want from the world,
division, subtraction, carry the one.

Half an hour later the plates gleam
in the rack like children fresh from a bath,
the upturned glasses like a wiser man's metaphor
for enlightenment, clarity and emptiness,
denial of the calculating self.
He turns out the light, counts the stairs
to his room, the necklace of stars framed
by the window over the bed.
He has never felt lonelier,
never so completely at home in his life.

ALE & BITTER

Your days a deliberate
measured excursion into loss.
Cigarettes disappearing from
the pack at your elbow,
three pale soldiers
to every pint of ale or bitter,
glasses emptied and set aside
like spent cartridges,
wet butt of each hour
stubbed and tossed,
your fingers stained nicotine yellow,
the same sullen shade
as the indoor light
that never changes.

A resolute, determined quitter,
pace steady as a metronome,
the copper facing around the bar
offers your reflection
in nostalgic sepia tone,
as if to say you're already most
of the way gone from here,
someone else's recollection.
Same forced march every night,
no variation, no turning.

You must hate to wake up
in the morning.

UNDONE

I want you to tie me up.

It was very late,
even the moon was asleep.

He tied her up.

Her face in the tight halo of
light from the bedside clock,
hands crossed at the wrists
behind her back.

He said, *Tell me what you want.*

Her smile then,
the sudden tug of it,
like a knot being
tested.

It was very late,
the stars about to be undone
by daylight.

After he slipped her hands free
she held him awhile,
could see he needed comforting.

A slow heat rising from
her skin where she touched him,
like the sun coming up.

STATIC

Shuck my clothes in the dark—
blue sparks click in
the charged fabric as I peel
a sweatshirt over my head
and a close-up of Mom and Dad
at the kitchen sink flickers by,
two brace of rabbit
on the counter for skinning—
I wasn't old enough to wield the knife,
watched the blade bracelet
the back paws, fur muffler
jacked off the carcass,
stripped clear of the head

The blood and offal stink
always drove me outside
but there was something beautiful
about the bared machinery
of those bodies,
grain of muscle taut
as guy wire over bone;
only the delicate fur cuffs
at the paw-tips made them
seem unfortunate,
and I've never felt so naked
going to bed alone as now,
picturing those cadavers
laid against porcelain,
the flesh dark as cedar

Shake out my clothes once more
for the comforting chatter
of static in the material,
its brief constellation of light

Running the Quidi Vidi loop in mauzy weather,
alone on the trail but for the vague outline of
a retriever trotting ahead,
arc of the tail's baton marking time.
A ballgame on the diamond at Caribou Field,
gauzy park lights visible on the opposite shore—
blunted *chink* of the metal bat making contact,
muffled commotion as a pop fly
disappears into grey-mesh sky,
teammates calling advice on distance,
direction, index fingers extended
pointlessly toward absence.
The one silent player is the outfielder
judging the ball's arc by its trajectory
as it leaves the bat
and I can feel the contours of
his solitude clear across the lake,
a loneliness made worse by company,
by the encouragement of others.

That edgeless shape of a dog
steadily ahead on the trail
and not appearing to belong to anyone.

BUSHED

On Round Lake, two hours north of North Bay

Cool July night, sodden grey tarp of cloud.
Shoreline tiered with trees in ragged rows,
wind lisping in the leaves like the subdued

murmur of a waiting audience
as we surrender shoes and summer clothes.
Count to three before rushing the cold,

whisky-chill kissing us everywhere at once—
our startled voices skim the water's palm
and sink into darkness like skipped stones.

Part of what you are leaks into the calm
and gets lost out here, the country fills
you up with strangeness. Woods ring the lake for miles,

but it feels like depth more than distance—
no surprise lone settlers found something willed
in the forest's silence that stripped them of sense,

plunged them naked into bottomless bush.
The water's boreal whisker bristles
against bare skin while in the black beneath us

splake and pickerel navigate currents
of startled and dimming human voices.
On the opposite shore, fireflies flash

some unbroken code in the underbrush.

FEVER

Big Island Cemetery, Prince Edward County, Ontario

Most of the headstones have long since collapsed,
moss and a tangled mesh of grasses obscuring
the carefully wrought names and dates,
the chiselled Victorian pieties that seem
trite and sadly implausible a century on.

Several clusters of marble testament
to a minor calamity that passed through
Loyalist country in 1885 and 86,
some indiscriminate disease moving from
family to family like a slash-and-burn
homesteader clearing brush,
old and young alike twisting in their beds
as if turning on a spit,
their senses so addled by fever
they didn't recognize the people
who tended them as they died.
When those who'd nursed the dead
took sick themselves, their heads were
scorched clean of the names and faces
they'd hardly had time to mourn.

How ancient those lives seem now,
ravaged and almost past remembering—
even God struggles to untangle the skein
of their voices from the stars,
to recall the simple clarity of prayers
that kept them awake at night,
their faces in lamplight dazzled with tears.

Barely a hundred years of forgetting in this field
and time beyond time to carry on forgetting,
and being forgotten.

Everyone these people once cared for is dead
and they haven't so much as turned in their beds.

NORTHERN LIGHTS, LOOKING BACK

We waded out into the damp air
to watch those enormous seines of light,
delicate mesh moored to the constant stars,
their drift and settle miming tides.

Standing beneath them we both felt stripped,
ambushed by awe and strangely heartsick—
cold and alone and lost in their wake
like two dim stars the sky had dropped.

The hard times were anchored miles off still—
it was just beauty that hooked and held our sight,
made us lonely for something that travelled
through our time like water sieving a net.

I didn't think to turn to watch your face
but, looking back, I wish I had. Our lives then
lit by the pitch of the sky's blind grace,
until night leant down to draw the light in.

ARTIFACTS

An old couple lived here before you and I.
Brother and sister, raised in this house,
forced home after years away
by a stingy pension, the death of a spouse.

They didn't get on at all in the end,
the neighbours say, led separate lives,
divided the six rooms between them,
ate separate meals at appointed times.

Stuffed in a drawer, we found sheets of paper
columned with scores, their names scrawled at the top—
they must have argued over words for years
till first the Scrabble, then the talking stopped.

A sad story told by sad artifacts
we never thought might spell out our own.
A house divided as if split by an axe.
Two people sitting to their meals alone.

He took his shift that night to keep company
with her dying, her breath clotted with fluid,
heart treading water in the cavity of her chest,
one hand flailing like a distress signal
he could only watch from his impossible distance.
Before dawn she vomited a mouthful
of black bile and left them to the morning's
muffled light gathering at the windows.

He watched from the doorway as a doctor
unpacked her stethoscope, surprised to register
her loveliness, the pulse of it brimming his head
as she nodded in time to the nothing she heard
of the stilled heart, as she scrawled a florid,
illegible signature on the death certificate.
The shrouded body strapped to a stretcher then
and wheeled through rain to the hearse,
black car drifting off into the raw mouth
of December weather, leaving them
to strip the bed, scour the soiled sheets.

A long dirty morning and no relief from it
but his time in the presence of the lovely doctor
when he was unfaithful to a fresh grief,
ashamed of the infidelity, and grateful to see
the beautiful survives what he will not.

BLUE IN GREEN (TAKE 2)

Hungover this morning
and slightly stoned on allergy pills,
I'm navigating a section of bright
countryside just north of nausea,
Bill Evans at his mellowest holding
the wheel and probably wrecked
as he played the black and tan melody,
all ten fingers intent as bees
drunk on honey sweetness.

Spring again, every green thing
slurring pollen into the blue
like a party of name-droppers
intoxicated by its own gossip,
the buzz of life in the air
so thick it's nearly audible.

The music makes me feel clumsy
with my time, it drifts off the map
without ever losing its way,
chords polished and carefully placed
like stones marking a path home,
like notes I'd like to write to myself:

You are exactly where you need to be.

Pay attention to everything.

It's good to be alive.

BLUE IN GREEN (TAKE 3)

Hungover this morning
and slightly stoned on
allergy pills,
I'm chasing the blue shade
of Bill Evans's hands
to keep the bright at bay,
music filtering sunlight
like a deep pool of water.

Julie turns toward me to say
I always wake up
thinking about food or sex
and this time of year
the world offers endless
improvisations on those themes.
Hard to explain jazz
or addiction with a notion
as simple as appetite,
but those variations
inhabit its frequency
the same as blue does green.

The music meadows the late hours
of the morning,
each note has the heft,
the pendulous grace of
bees in flight—
too heavy for their wings,
they're kept aloft by desire,
by their hunger for life.

VIEW OF THE MOON FROM THE DECK
BUILT ABOVE HIS KITCHEN

Constructed by some amateur unconcerned
with the finer details of carpentry, with consequences,
joists laid a foot too wide so the boards bow
beneath the weight of a body, the corner posts
sunk into the roof and poorly sealed with pitch,
ceiling plaster blistered by rainwater seeping
through leaks too insidious to trace,
and no hope of putting it right without taking
the whole goddamn thing down.

The moon nearly full across the harbour,
blue weight of the Southside Hills bowed
in darkness beneath it.

The rain getting in.

UNDER
THE KEEL
2013

On a short haul flight to Boston
with *The Selected Paul Durcan*,
Irish lines conjuring the Catholic
girl who taught me to neck—
her mouth a marriage of cigarettes
and Wrigley's spearmint,
my hands two raw cadets
assigned their permanent
station: the blue denim
circling those extravagant hips.

And younger, stalking minnows
in a pond set among spruce
trees beside the Catholic manse;
the handsome Father who
played tennis in white shoes,
who flew his own plane,
and eventually renounced
the priesthood for a woman.

All the way to Logan
International, the twinge
of something left behind
at the airport in Halifax
while waiting for my connection,
a loss I can't coax
clear of faint apprehension.
The stewardess leans in
to offer a tray of snacks,
a small silver crucifix

tick-tocking below her perfect
smile, one immaculate hand
marred by the fleck
of a gold wedding band.

A corrupted brook that filtered through bog
beside the mill, a glittering trough of mine
tailings whose narrow passage halved the town,
its muddy verge and surface iridescent
with arsenic and sulphur and ore slag.

It was a lit cigarette, a tropical plant
in a coniferous landscape, and we spent
hours soaking our shoes in the toxic sog,
floating sticks and seedpods on the current,
mucking bare-handed in the auroral brine.

It was a honeyed channel, an oily serpent
urging against an explicit parental ban—
we suffered their discipline without complaint,
made promises knowing we would renege
for the water's radiance, its poisonous sheen.

BOYS

Not old enough to pay for our trouble,
or even name it, we wandered the town

after dark like dogs, half-tamed at best.
We set small fires and hurled rocks and pissed

against school doors, nosing the margin
of the disallowed, the out of bounds.

We ranged as far as the train trestle,
sniffing underbrush and the long grass

for anything dead or lost or unusual,
broke into empty buildings for the thrill

of stealing through forbidden spaces,
of standing at darkened windows, invisible

while the innocent traffic drove past.
We perched at the lip of change, we knew it,

though in our eyes time itself stood still,
we couldn't imagine ourselves at thirty

or married or living other places—
what we wanted was to see the world undress,

to lie down naked somewhere dirty
and fuck, to do all the unspeakable

things our green minds could only intuit,
a communal urge we suffered alone.

Half-grown, we were living our life by halves,
our dreams were vacant rooms we didn't own

and roamed in silence, shadows behind dark glass,
our mute hearts a mystery to ourselves.

GIRLS

Their bodies were stripling and sleek
and more or less like our own

but for the one alien nook
that made them partial to skirts

and the Easy-bake oven,
clumsy with a hockey stick—

it was the only explanation
the world offered for their eccentric

habits, their feminine quirks,
and it was too simple and stark

a truth to be refuted—
you stood or sat to take a piss

which was the final word on
how a soul was constituted.

Even the beauties who were rough
and tumble, who were known to pick

a fight and could use their fists
carried that internal question mark,

a riddle we couldn't solve or evade.
They were a fruitless provocation,

a rattling kernel of magic
we pretended did not exist,

ten years old and already afraid
we'd never get far enough

inside that cleft's niggling divide
to understand what makes them tick.

COCK TEASE

She had a raw mouth for twelve,
barely-there breasts and a name that made
her reckless and surly by turns.

She liked to be touched and could see
it might be her undoing, she fended off
advances with a savage fatalism

or shifted just out of reach like a sunbather
avoiding a creeping block of shade.
It was wrong to want the kind of attention

boys were willing to give her
and she circled as close as she could
without brushing against it,

she brushed against it with her eyes
averted before startling away
like something scalded.

I was embarrassed to court
her company but risked the taint
for her reputation's promise,

hand working beneath her cotton shirt,
fingers grazing the surprising length
of a nipple before she bolted,

though never far enough to shut the door
completely. That crude tug of war
was everything on offer between us

and we chafed against each
other with a sour sort
of affection.

My last summer we hung out at Fong's
restaurant, at the penstock or the Mud Hole,
waiting for something to happen,
drove aimlessly through town with Albert

who was seventeen and worked part-
time to cover his gas, his hash, his beer.
His girlfriend scooched toward the gear
shift to make room as we climbed in

to troll the quiet streets an hour
with all the car windows down,
the radio high enough we had to shout
to be heard above the incandescent,

sugary marl of the latest hit songs.
The girlfriend was blonde and slender
which was enough to pass for beautiful
in a backwater town that small

and Albert shocked us by dumping her
in August. "She wouldn't even give
me a bit of finger skin," was his rationale
and we didn't ask for more detail,

though I'd never heard the term before
and had to guess at what it meant.
Nothing much happened in those final
weeks, beyond our slow meander

through the streets I was about to leave
for good, almost fourteen and still a virgin—
more profoundly so, it turned out,
than I'd even considered possible.

TUSK

They gimped into town
driving geriatric trucks,
circled their rinky-dink
convoy on the softball
field's faded diamond,
a duct-taped carnival
of slapstick clowns,
a clutch of dismal
animal acts.
They were a grim crowd,
setting up in the next
dog-eared company hole
down a dead-end road,
barking at the little fucks
who descended to gawk
inside their mobile
homes, to watch them unload,
then stake and pole
a withered circus tent.

Nosed out the main event
before the show began,
a small, squat elephant
chained in a makeshift
stall behind a trailer,
the behemoth no taller
than myself at ten.
Wary, intelligent
eyes above a single rail,
the absurdly deft

prehensile trunk
climbing shyly
in my direction—
it took all my mettle
to meet the gesture
halfway, to barehand
that whiskered husk,
so alien and animate
my arm reared
back like I'd been shot.

It was missing one
stubby yellow tusk,
a sad asymmetry
that each day afterward
I somehow felt
was more and more my fault.

FOX ON THE FUNK ISLANDS

She drifted down from the Strait on an ice pan
and played havoc with the breeding season,

the only predator within fifty miles—
wandering the well-stocked aisles,

chasing seabirds off their roosts for the tasty
morsel of fresh eggs, gorging on the delicacy,

and she killed a freezer-load of adults as well,
caching the carcasses she was too full

to eat, an ancient northern instinct, a store
against the meagre months of winter.

We gave her no chance on the Funks
after the colony migrated, thinking once

snow settled in on that deserted ground
she would starve to death or drown

in the bottomless cold, too rich
an appetite for an economy so strict,

but she was waiting for us in June
having survived the winter dark alone,

making a long celebratory meal
of anything she could chase down and kill.

The returning birds unsettled, too skittish
to lay or tend their chicks in the nest,

and all summer we set traps, hoping to take
her alive; each time she stole the bait,

leaving some small gift in trade,
a razorbill's head, a puffin's wing laid

beside the trigger inside the useless device
as a thank you or a taunt, and once or twice

a week she hung near the camp to watch us,
her stare calm and intently curious.

We were an inconsequential riddle
on the margins of her concern, an idle

interest indulged at her leisure,
and what she made of us being there

preoccupied our talk as we picked away
at the summer's banding survey,

imagining ourselves in her predicament,
anomalous and intransigent,

wild and sovereign, hopelessly astray—
and we admired the creature, grudgingly.

Shot her our last week out there before the boat
arrived, and we each laid a hand to the ratty coat

as if to apologize for the necessary offence,
a gesture of awkward, amoral reverence.

MINKE WHALE IN SLO-MO

A dark patch of ocean blisters up near
the gunwale with alien deliberation,

sea-water on the rising surface crackling
and receding like celluloid snared in

a projector's heat before the grappling
hook of the dorsal fin enters the frame,

pinning the shapeless shape to a name,
to identifiable attributes and traits,

the yellow dory jarred by the collision
then rocking back as the minke shears

down and away and disappears
like a drunk driver fleeing a minor

accident through backroads, deserted streets.
Repeat the thirty-second clip a dozen

times for the little mystery's slow-motion
resolve, for that rough kiss so impulsive

and unexpected it leaves the diminutive
wooden boat shaking on the ocean.

Dumped and torched in the White Hills decades back
and everything remotely organic—
cushions, tires and vinyl, interior fabric—
long ago stripped from the scrawny wreck
by fire, by decay's reckoning *tick tick tick*.
All year it squats there, listing off the track
in the approximate shape of a ransacked
four-door sedan with automatic
transmission, though each season the trick
is less convincing and that rusting lock,
soon enough, will be impossible to pick.

Meantime, the woods improvise a meadow
in its coldframe, seeding the import's hollow
shell with alder, with fern and willow,
all craning their heads out a window
or doors hanging ajar, a wayward crew
on a summer road trip, the Datsun's slow
collapse just countryside they're passing through.

BURN BARREL

Halfway out the yard
an ancient barrel once
used as incinerator
for scrap wood and garden
waste, its face obscured
by a skirt of spent grass
and raspberry canes.
The teacher who scarred
my father's youth
with math and grammar
and Alfred, Lord Tennyson
lived somewhere in the pasture
beyond the back fence,
though the house is long gone,
passed into oblivion
as if fed board by board
to the barrel's mouth.
Dad could still recite
those Victorian verses
his last months alive
and there seems some truth
in that, half-realized,
a lesson whose little light
blooms and dies back each season
and can't be seen entire,
though it was just a party trick
in my father's eyes.
Behind the grassy screen
the barrel is so thick
with rust it's porous,

eaten through by salt air
and by something kin
to its own blind appetite—
time's slow, smokeless fire.

QUESTIONS OF TRAVEL

. . . the choice is never wide and never free.
    —Elizabeth Bishop

After her mother lost her mind
she was shunted among family
in Nova Scotia and New England,

a little wandering heirloom,
a great-uncle's postcard painting
no one could bear to throw away,

hanging awhile in a back room
before being consigned
to some relative's steamer trunk.

In college she turned to poetry,
then to wanderlust and drink,
but as a child there was no respite

and she rebelled by making herself ill
with asthma and constipation,
with spells of vertigo or fainting,

her protest passive and internal—
tucked her head under sheets at night,
the only soul awake in Worcester

as she signalled SOS with a flashlight,
and that early miniature
managed to contain

every landscape yet to come.
She grew up a curious creature,
writing as if she were certain

that something out there loves us all,
but never completely at home
in the world, never married

for long to a single place or person—
she travelled to escape the fear
she was her mother's daughter,

to have something useful
to do with the baggage she carried,
to keep her buried head above water.

DEADFALL

At the old farm garden with John Fitzgerald,
sunlight in the copse of trees filtered green

and liquid as light through an aquarium,
beams of birch and spruce brought down

by wind and going to rot where they fell—
it gives the droke the feel of a building

abandoned and falling into ruin
at the edge of a derelict field

overgrown with wild rose and bramble.
Stand clear when Johnny wields

the chainsaw, pintailing chips and bark
like sparks showering off a welding

torch as he limbs out the deadfall
and skins the punky rind from

lengths still solid enough to burn.
My job is to drag the logs he's milled

to a quad and four-post trailer parked
where bush encroaches on the garden,

to clear the sheared scrag in his wake,
to suggest likely candidates among

the sticks of firewood composting
on forest floor or caught up in

the hammock of neighbouring branches,
though it's hard to guess what we can take

by looking, the rot flares at the core
and smoulders outward ring by ring.

Tempted to make something more
of that detail squatting on its haunches

in the underwater light as we work
but John would only shake his head

at the conceits I entertain on the side.
My job is hauling and stacking wood.

It's simple waste he can't abide.

A STONE

When her husband died she placed a gravestone
with her name and birthdate next his own,

a blank left to mark the day she'd be gone
from the world, took each morning on loan

and managed twenty years with afternoon
soaps, *Wheel of Fortune*, the rotary phone.

That empty space like a Buddhist koan,
the sound of one hand clapping, something sewn

into a coat's lining and forgotten
in a basement closet, a rock she'd thrown

so hard and high she couldn't have known
where or when it might come down.

That shrouded date was the Lord's dominion
and she wore it like an invisible crown.

This is my kitchen, mine and Gasker's. Him with the hands
on his knees like he's about to help himself to his feet. Even
set still he seems on his way to some bit of work or other. But
that's only show these days. Can't get out of his own way most
of the time, spends his nights turning like a spindle on a
lathe, the aches working at him. He got old of a sudden and I
never saw it coming.

There's people claim the second sight and I count myself
lucky to have the first. Twenty-seven when my sister died.
Gasker left with two young ones and I never saw it coming all
the same, him proposing. Not the marrying kind was what
people said, and me along with them. Aunt Annie set me on
Mother's stomach when I was born and said, Put a pair of
boots on that one, Sarah, she's ready for the woods.

That one over there is my daughter Patience. First child
of my own. I had no time for youngsters in those days and I
thought it would be a nice reminder. It's hard to stand in the
middle of a room yelling *Patience!* without feeling like a fool.

It didn't always work. But nothing ever does.

She still got the look of it about her. Like the firmament
could fall into the ocean and her with the hands folded in her
lap like that, calm as you please.

Don't mind the dress and apron on me, I was never
happier than in the backcountry hauling wood or setting
snares or picking berries in over the barrens. Can't be at that
sort of business now though, Gasker the way he is. And
sitting don't bother me like it used to. Had near enough of life
to do me, I guess. In my mind I'm still knocking around in
the woods most of the time I sit by this window, washing out
in the light.

This is the kitchen, like I said. First time I ever set for a photograph. Some American stopping in on the coastal boat. I thought the man was simple is the truth of it, ducking in behind that box of his, waving at us to hold still. If I'd known it would mean being gawked at by you crowd I'd have told him to put the machine away, sit to a cup of tea like a sensible person.

Saved myself all this gabbing.

WATERMARK

Pentecostal Baptism, Catalina ca. 1940

1.

Place the tips of my shoes
at the ocean's lip
so I can hold my Bible
out over the surface
Spirit of God moving on the water
Brother Harold up to his arse
in the shallows
salt riming the nap
of his Sunday trousers

There's some suggest
these annual baptisms
be shifted to a pond
on the barrens
made more hospitable
by three months of summer heat—
I say Get behind me Satan,
the ocean is where God's sorrows
reside in the world
a wilderness to pierce
the heart of the lost
if they want comfort let them
join the Sally Ann

The penitents walk into the harbour
where Brother Harold
awaits them in tie and suspenders
and banker's spectacles
solemn as an executioner—
drowns each sinner
in the stinging cold
and they rise up shriven
aquiver with the Lord in their veins
forever and ever
amen

2.

you hears the Lord
when Mr. Scaines holds
your head beneath the water
that's what I was told,
a voice ringing from the other side
of the tide's mauzy drone

it's like a mother speaking aloud
while you're still part of her
Dorcas Pottle said,
before you come wholly
into the world of sin
before you're wholly alone

kept my eyes wide
while I was under
as if that would help me hear,
as if to let Jesus enter by
any door He might
but the ocean stopped my ears
or I was deafened by some fault
of my own
and lifted into the light
with neither word to carry

forsaken is how I felt—
fell against the hands at my side
wanting to fight,
wanting to be lowered back down

eyes burning out of my head
with the water's salt

3.

washed in the blood
of the lamb amen,
I wants a good dunking
right enough

brothers and sisters
I spent half me days
in drinking
and the other half
repenting of it—
like sculling out
to an empty trap
and home again,
all's to show for your trip
is blisters

bloody great shock
of the water every time,
so cold going under
it's like being shorn
front and back
with a rusty blade,
surprised there's no scars
to tell the scouring

only down a second
before Harold Scaines
hauls you out by the armpits
but I never felt so clean
as coming up into the glow
of those faces attending

on the landwash,
all praying for my sake

I been sove three times now

please God this one will take

CAUSE OF DEATH AND REMARKS

from Jerrett's Genealogy, Provincial Archives

Died suddenly. Died young.
Fell overboard and drowned.
Boat capsized while hunting loons,
body never found.

Lived one hour.
Lived with brother George.
Lost on schooner coming from St. John's
with all hands on board.

Jaundice. Senility. Apoplexy.
Died in First World War.
Died fishing on the Labrador.
Joined Salvation Army.

Tuberculosis. Influenza.
Multiple myeloma.
Must have died young,
not remembered by sister Julia.

Died of old age. Pleuritis.
Coronary thrombosis.
Operated Post Office
at Cavendish.

MARK WATERMAN, LIGHTKEEPER (RETIRED), ADDRESSES HIS SUCCESSOR CA. 1931

So this is Rag's Island,
she's yours now and welcome.

Thought I might have a few words
to hold you in good stead

some small bit of wisdom
but I'm starting to have me doubts.

Keep yourself occupied
or the place will mozzle your head

send you gabbling about
the cliffs after the birds.

My first winter I heard
voices adrift in the wind

sat awake for days on end
scribbling notes of what was said

before I come to my senses.
Go on and laugh, it sounds

like so much foolishness
to someone just come aboard.

All told the life's not that bad.
The Duty chart's a fair guide

of what the job asks of a man.
Drink as much as you can afford.

Any more I could think to add
you're too green to understand.

STARS ON THE WATER

February and a savage night
to be out, wind eighty knots,

waves cresting fifty feet,
a body would last only minutes

adrift in that ocean
but we went looking regardless.

The lifeboat was red fibreglass,
white plastic tarp for a cabin,

now and again a light would flash
inside so you knew there was men

aboard, though in what condition
or how many you couldn't guess.

A second vessel worked close
enough to heave them a line

and we counted eight or nine
in lifejackets over street clothes,

more again huddled at the back.
Lost sight of them in a trough

just as they tipped into the bleak
and the men pitched from the raft—

we come over the wave's peak
and those life-vest locator

lights were like stars on the water.
Didn't have the heart to figure

numbers against the black
but we were close enough to hear

them calling and pretended
we might manage a rescue still,

flinging our boat hooks from the rail
as if our own lives depended

on the show. You had to try it
even so you knew how things ended.

Carried on a long while
after the last of them went quiet.

THE STARS, AFTER JOHN'S HOMEBREW

He carts them up from the basement
two at a time, empties each green bottle

into a measuring cup, slow-pours your glass
to siphon off the gravelly sediment.

Bitter fizz in the nose that doesn't last,
a gnarly blend of sour green apple

and sugar, a finish that would throttle
the song of a hermit thrush.

"Another drop of the WD-70?"
he asks halfway through your first

when one is more than plenty—
the second a patch of stinging nettle

with a briny gasoline undertone
and the subtlest hint of immortality,

the third enough to plant you face down
among the spuds in Johnny's garden.

May as well have another this far in,
his wife won't let you chance the car

even after you sober up a little
on a lunch of molasses bread and tea,

you'll have to stagger around the harbour
with the ocean's sweet nothing in your ears,

and the stars, lord jesus, the stars!
the grit of sediment beginning to settle

in night's enormous still, their thorny glare
rattling the dark like a length of sheet-metal.

HOPE CHEST

Something Old

Shale foundation and a drainpipe's dead
stump dwarfed by seedling pine and alder
rising through the ghost of floorboard

and swept canvas. A concrete step where
the backdoor once opened onto Nan's yard
still overlooked by the lilac that held her

dark-panelled hallway in shades of shade
all summer; laden with blossoms each June,
branches swaying into waist-high grass

under the weight of a sweetness
too flagrant to last. Might have considered
the same true of us when we began,

lavish haze flowering from every gesture,
the kind of extravagance that can floor
the senses and keeps less than a season,

but the world will make a stranger
of the most obvious expectation.
Couldn't have guessed, those childhood

vacations I slept in an upstairs room,
that what seemed most sound and certain
about the property would disappear

and the lilac endure in its absence,
spilling out over the ancient fence,
palings foundering beneath the bloom.

Something New

When test results confirmed what we feared
Dad was moved to the terminal ward

and my mother rarely left his side,
all day to help him to and from his bed,

to wash and feed him, rub his calves
and feet, and she stayed there half

the nights as well, wouldn't give in to sleep,
sat up in a chair so she could keep

tabs on any sound or motion from
her husband lying across the room.

Her nights at home I stayed with Dad,
but once he'd taken his evening meds

I slept through till morning unless he called.
Weeks into that shiftwork before he told

me the sleeping pills leached clear
of his system in the loneliest hours

and he lay quiet at three and four
so as not to disturb his company,

dead to the world on a cot near the floor.
I could never match Mom's fidelity

to the vigil, admired it from a distance
that seemed a lack in me, a resistance

I've always felt to risking love,
the cut of it that goes hand in glove

with tying yourself to something as frail
as another person. Bound to fail

was my thought and I always managed
to keep well clear, but my parents' marriage

in its final days on the cancer ward
made me think I'd lived my life a coward.

Not the most romantic lines
to preface a wedding declaration

but I don't know how else to name
the place I started from, to frame

how new this is, believing we're equal
to what the world might offer or steal

from us in the time we're given.
We're not young enough to ask for heaven

on earth, but here's a promise I will make —
to stay by you, to be fully awake.

Something Borrowed

An apple you left on my desk
a month ago or longer—
bruises dimple the crown,
but the red circumference
is still as firm as a fist.

Every day I shift it among
books and receipts, shopping lists,
like a subway passenger
half asleep underground,
shunted station to station.

Always I lift and set it down
carefully by the stem.
Can just resist the temptation
to lick your fingerprints
off its nearly flawless skin.

Something Blues

You better come on in my kitchen,
cause it's going to be raining outdoors
    —Robert Johnson

Almost quit before I met you,
didn't sit up nights by the phone,
I was halfways gone to believing
I'd be better off on my own,
I came on in a few kitchens
and hummed a few bars of that song—
it wasn't love, it just kept me busy
until you came along.

I've driven this block a time or two
but I never gave up the keys,
always kept one foot out the door
so I could hightail it when I pleased,
I came on in a few kitchens
where everything right went wrong—
it wasn't love, it just kept me busy
until you came along.

[bridge]

Didn't know it was you I was missing
when I went out on the town,
tried to tell myself I was serious
when I was just messing around,
fell into some cool clear water
but it never ran deep enough,
Lord, it was something,
but it wasn't love.

Almost quit before I met you,
didn't sit up nights by the phone,
I was halfways gone to believing
I'd be better off on my own,
I came on in a few kitchens
but I never stayed in there long—
it wasn't love, it just kept me busy
until you came along.

Unplug the insatiable telephone,
the apocalypse unfolding hourly
on the network news crawl.

Ignore the kitchen's Victorian factory
of filthy dishes, the laundry pile
suffocating a lost child in the basement.

Ignore the lost children.
Forget music and saffron and oysters,
put aside the clichéd, the quaint

rituals of wine and lingerie—
aphrodisiacs are for amateurs
with more time than common sense,

who've yet to learn bliss is stolen
from the world in small, piercing slivers.
Think of stealth as foreplay

in the prison yard of daily events,
sneak out of your clothes
as soon as the coast is clear—

the air raid siren of a youngster
crying is about to rise
through the bedroom floor,

the weight of the Three Gorges reservoir
has altered the planet's rotation
by the same rate at which yesterday's

dishes are going septic in the sink—
be resolute. Bliss lives for bliss alone,
apply yourself to that ephemeral sliver.

You have less time than you think.

THE GANGES, AT MIDDLE AGE

They stopped on the walkway
below my living room window,

spent fifteen minutes making out
on concrete steps in the dark

oblivious to the cold and wet,
pausing occasionally to check

the time, talking together in low
voices about god knows what,

love or ontology or a curfew
they were wearing at the fringes.

Can't recall what woke me
or why I left my bed to brood

here in the gloom, insomniac,
some creaky hinge of middle age,

the kind of worry that changes
nothing, makes us voyeurs

of our own lame circumstances,
the roof maybe, the mortgage,

the uneasy sense of drift and decay
that dogs the night's smallest hours.

Heard them before I could pick
any detail clear of shadow

and not much surfaced through the murk,
couldn't see where hands were busy

or what buttons were undone,
but the physical intimacy

was raw, almost pornographic,
they might have been eating food

off each others' naked skin—
felt like a dirty old prick

spying on the private ceremony
but couldn't make myself look away.

I watched those anonymous pilgrims dive
into the foul water of the Ganges

as if touched by something holy
a moment that went on for ages,

blissful both, arrayed with flowers,
before meandering downstream slowly

toward the lights on Highland Drive.

THE LANDING

Ten years he's been dead when I find my
self engaged in some extracurricular
with two girls who seem, on the face of things,
not quite old enough to buy their own liquor.

The slight brunette saunters off to powder
her nose, adorned only in pearl earrings,
but she hesitates at the door, spooked by
the knell of footsteps ringing up the stair,

and I'm ushered out to meet the intruder—
my father, circa his days at the mill,
shapeless work shirt, a wisp of thinning hair,
the walrus moustache still black as coal.

"It's my Dad," I tell the girls and stare
as the deliberate figure comes to rest
shy of the landing on the top floor,
his dark eyes glassy and expressionless.

"It's just a dream," I announce to no one,
alone with him now and wanting free
of whatever compulsion conjured the man,
grief or bald shame or some muddier charm

delivering that absence within one arm
length, one step down the ancient stairway.
Our lives are simpler than we care to see.
Even in the thorniest circumstance,

we dismiss the heart as a mystery
to avoid ourselves or, worse, put make-up
on a pig, to use my father's term.
He lingers there in a familiar silence,

never much for reprimand or handing
out advice, but he seems not to know his own
flesh and when I step off the landing
to reach for him, of course, I wake up.

UNDER SILK

My wife is dead, is dead, is dead
and I'm crawling a cold hardwood
hallway bawling to beat the band
when I come to myself in bed,
darkened room rising piecemeal
to a grey light: bookcase, nightstand,
the duvet cover we purchased
while passing through Rajasthan,
Holly under silk beside me,
her breath a calm surf that dresses
and undresses its stretch of sand,
and I'm struck by the strangeness
in that inscrutable syllable
wife, its veiled etymology,
that medieval stone fortress
moated and wreathed in mist—
whisper the word like a spell
from a cryptic German fable,
picking at the dream's surface
as if its details were a scab grown
over a truth more elusive,
the widowed hunchback all the while
keening like some inconsolable
ancient on a forsaken beach,
full fathoms beyond the solace
of language, of human speech.

2.

We'd strolled down into Jodhpur
from the heights of a fairytale
castle where successive Moghuls
layered their filigreed courts one
on another like sediment
settling in elaborate moulds,
each set of narrow marble stairs
a portal between the ages,
as if to teach time's long lesson
in the space of an afternoon.
Dusk before we found the merchant
near the market's clock tower,
eight ramshackle flights honeycombed
with the incongruous splendour
of pashmina and cotton,
of handwoven carpets and shawls
displayed by a fey, shoeless salesman
who parachuted his wares'
raw silk and organza at our feet,
so much beauty it seemed unfair
we could have it for so little,
each item settling to the floor
with the stiff, textured rustle
of wet paper dried in sunlight,
and we leafed through them like pages
recovered from an ocean current,
the fugitive words lost to sight
but still faintly, faintly there.

NEW
POEMS

50

1.

You've watched it come this way for miles, intent,
decided, the barely perceptible limp in its gait

like a mild stutter, the kind of speech impediment
a child, given time, might learn to escape.

It's toting a plain cardboard box meant
for you, the flaps folded shut without tape.

2.

Near enough now to see the dog-eared look on its face
like something borrowed from a public library,
something thumbed through ten thousand times.

It's wearing a not-quite-stylish jacket
much like the one you donated to charity
as you said good-bye to your twenties—

a coat you were on the fence about letting
go, and seeing it again you are still of two minds.
A hand rises out of the sleeve in greeting

and you wave back, out of habit.

3.

That cardboard box is the thing.
The cagey half a century
that has gone into packing
and carting it to this address.

You can't begin to guess
at the myriad inevitable
coiled like a roll of cash
in the coffer's darkness,

all of it yours to carry.
The unmarked box just small
enough to hold something hellish,
something indelible.

YIELD

My wife is in the field,
scouting a proposed route
for transmission towers,
sent ahead of the engineers
through bird habitat
earmarked to funnel Labrador's
bridled electrical yield
across bog and scrub forest
and broken escarpment
to feed our iPods, our toasters.
Muled under wet gear and tent,
she is parsing the ferment
for a singular eddy of grass,
a thumbnail afloat
on a churn of wilderness,
like some resolute
Romantic poet in pursuit
of a metaphor to best
all nightingale metaphors.

What powers the world is guile
and grit and happenstance—
Nature surrenders nothing by
design and little by chance,
each cup and saucer concealed
with a cunning distilled
by trial and error's
feral ingenuity.
My wife's left hand for scale
in her photos, the nest

palming its eggs like ballast
meant to settle the keel,
to keep that weightless vessel
riding trim and steady
in the current's murky pull.

THE COMMITMENTS

My wife is at sea, perched inside the glassed ledge
of a coast guard ship during daylight hours,
reckoning seabirds encountered while underway,
dropping data into the wake of a computer's
steadily widening intelligence.

Her evenings aboard are hazier affairs,
tax-free wine, a beer-choked bar fridge,
a windowless lounge for satellite hockey,
for small-stakes crib tournaments
among the science crew and officers,

a foreign culture she describes to me
in drunken emails that make little sense,
or make a sense I'm ill-equipped to judge.
Everything familiar in the woman slips free
of its moorings now and then, an immense

strangeness settles over the commitments
we live by. A trickster in the program embeds
this solitary watch, a distance that remains
as the smallest details of our days converge,
as a rising sea of zeros and ones

swallows our world and all it contains.

The weeks he worked at the mill 8 to 4
Dad deked home by way of the Union Hall
to stand his shift a round in the lull

before supper, hustling cross-town to preside
over grace, doling out our daily bread
with a little glow on, a devil's smile,

sneaking morsels from everyone's meal
while our heads were turned, making off-colour
proposals to our mother that we were

too young to grasp in their prurient detail
though the gist came through in her dismissal—
saucy, fondly annoyed. They both seemed more

or less content with their lot, I'd have said,
if a mirrored smile is any measure.
Only once was he late through the door,

crutched in on a shift-mate's staggered feet,
dumped and steadied in his waiting seat
where he bawled and listed hard to one side

while his sons stared and the half-eaten food
on our plates went cold. We were terrified
to see him so undone he couldn't speak,

unable to pry his eyes from the floor
even as Mom tried to coax him back
to sense, to all he asked of pleasure—

the kitchen's fare, his young wife, fatherhood.
It seemed more than alcohol that crippled
the man, some omen of teeming failure,

and nothing he owned could staunch the flood
that swarmed through and made him look a stranger,
foundering in front of his own flesh and blood.

It was a mother's instinct to protect
her kids that placed us under a neighbour's care
while she poured her husband into the car,

drove the blacktop to a gravel detour
ravelled through woods above Red Indian Lake
and they spent most of the evening there

watching the water's strobing white caps,
the sight like static on a radio's wave,
almost a comfort, a murmuring salve

as they waited for the jag's ragged kick
to break, for fatigue to shut off the taps.
There was no row, no needling the lapse,

as if my mother somehow understood
it was just the void peeking through a tear
in the day's fabric that ailed her passenger,

the stone stare of all we stand to lose while
our heads are turned, that dark lull we disregard
though the gist beds in our hearts like a seed

and blooms on occasion in bald detail.
My brothers and I were already sound
by the time they idled back to town,

rattled and wrung out, but undamaged.
Nothing was the same, except what mattered.
They had a life to be lived. They managed.

RED INDIAN LAKE

The Lake never took to heat—
even through August the shallows
hurt the bones in our feet
and we didn't go all the way in,
just paddled around until
we couldn't feel our toes.

The dam at its northern end
raised and lowered the water's reach,
stranding rafts of pulp bound
for the Grand Falls paper mill
on the highest stretch of beach;
by the book, it was illegal

to take those logs as salvage
but we helped our father poach
company property by the cord,
sawed and junked and stored
the plundered wood in plain view
along the lee-side cabin wall.

We wore the theft as a badge
of honour, a public declaration
that we owned the water and all
its contents simply by virtue
of time spent on the shore.
When the winter lake caught over

we skated the black ice for miles,
rifling as far as Buchans Island
with our coats spread for sails,
tacking home against the wind
that slowed us to a killing crawl.
Thawed our mortified flesh

at a fire fed by contraband,
shocked each time to feel it fresh—
life returning raw to each hand
and foot, a savage electrical
sting enough to make us bawl
and almost wish them dead again.

It was where ugly thrived.
Blight and galloping stench
prospered there in exile.

The spent and defective arrived
in the bed of a flagging half-ton
on a strict bi-weekly schedule.

A way station between town
and abiding absence,
a parcel of magic and ruin

we haunted all summer,
casting through that wild acre
of refuse in our young skin,

gleaming like crows.
We trawled hours through those
reeking ponds of junk

where the rarest prize—
porno mags or pocketknives—
could fairly make me sing.

Rats and the eternal stink
kept everyone but us well clear,
it was the only place in our lives

I felt like a king.

CHILDISH THINGS

Three times I tried to kill my brother
in a fistfight, thrashing blind and inured
to pain or remorse in the moment.

Smoked stolen cigarettes in a strike shack
tucked away near the Catholic graveyard,
choking stoically on each poisonous snake.

In older company I downed a six-pack
of O'Keefe's Extra Old Stock and spent
the night in misery, the puking so violent

and prolonged I half-expected to croak,
swore never to drink another
and kept the vow for most of a week.

Impossible to fix how far back it went,
that urge to raze the bordered
world—my first pennies laid on the track

to see them flattened as a train ripped past,
erasing that prim image of the Queen,
the new coins hot and smooth as glass.

I could sense there was an invisible line
where childish things were left behind
and I was clawing wildly in the black,

wanting to cross over, whatever the cost.

The odd Friday we could finagle
stewardship of someone's family car
we drove an hour across the border
to the brasserie in Fermont
where no one bothered about ID—
six Anglo kids at a scarred table
downing pitchers of Labatt 50,
the designated driver on his third
or fourth run through the one pint
he'd pledged his sole indulgence.
The longer we were ignored
the more at ease we felt there,
and we ordered the beer in French
after the first shy rounds—"Cinquante!"—
feeling drunkenly bilingual
on the strength of a single word.
Hustled to the car after last call,
bivering in that icebox while the heater
hacked a peephole through frost,
shouting uselessly to hurry the process
along. We were the only vehicle
travelling in either direction
and could have straddled the centre
line all the way home to Labrador,
the driver killing our headlights
on straightaways just to tempt the fates.
Blacktop hemmed by a ragged fence
of spruce and snow's endless ashen
blue, those winters seemed eternal
while they lasted, the landscape cursed,

though nothing of real consequence
occupied the adolescent forest
we motored through in slow motion,
which is why I remember so little
of those years, of what was spoken
or who we were, or where we guessed
our bottled ambitions might lead us—
we wanted everything the horizon
suggested was within our reach
which from this end of the glass
looks like nothing very much.

He was the most exotic
creature I'd ever met,
corpulent and balding
in a suit and tie, waddling
through the vacant parking lot
with one hand raised to hail
me across the quiet street,
as if I was a cab idling
in Manhattan traffic—
a native-born New Yorker,
fresh from the airport or
just through his first grim
night at the Grenfell Hotel,
his girth and lumbering gait
suggesting he'd made a meal
of a small to middling
American state
en route to Labrador.
All that stood between him
and endless arctic tundra
was an anemic shopping mall,
a tin-can hockey arena,
and that see-through skim
triggered a silent alarm
in the man, something befuddling
inspired him to flail
helplessly with his hailing arm
as he tweedledummed on a swivel,
taking the riddle in—
roads that dead-ended and nowhered

in the Big Land's navel,
company houses bordered
on all sides by a void
from an old wives' tale.
Nothing he knew compared
to the lack my hometown tried
to huckster off as charm.
Nothing had ever made him feel
so unaccountably small.

DOGBERRIES

They seemed a prodigal waste,
hanging off the trees in tight bouquets,

so irredeemably sour
even the jays refused to touch

them before the end of November
when there was nothing else

in the world to scavenge for.
We picked what we could reach,

pockets brimmed with berries we used
as ammunition, pelting innocent

bystanders or whipping them at each
other, the blood-bright nubs raising welts

on any patch of skin exposed—
hands and necks, the always naked face.

Bumper crops were a warning sign,
a useless surfeit said to augur

heavy weather, relentless frost,
months of misery and torment,

but the berries seemed immune
to the winters they forecast,

each tiny lamp holding its glow
through Halloween, then Christmas,

looking festively persistent
beneath their crooked caps of snow.

APRIL RETRIEVER

Winter on the cross
and plumes of dog shit
rising through snow's
sour retreat.

At this early stage
the cruel season
is seedy plumage,
blistered, seeping skin.

On a clear section
of gravel road,
the Lab happily rolls
in something dead.

BOXERS

Months since we'd met on this trail,
I'd assumed the old man had passed.

"Open heart surgery," he confessed,
titanium replacing a leaky valve.

We were the slightest of friends,
exchanging nods and careful pleasantries

while the dogs growled and feinted
and nosed each others' rear ends,

and it was unsettling to have a real
intimacy slip past the sentries,

a detail too nakedly confidential
for a near-stranger to bottle and shelve.

("Never married," he once volunteered,
proudly, as if he thought his life untainted,

as if love were a corrupting disease
he'd been spared by sheer force of will.

Posturing, I thought, swaggering denial,
but we weren't well-enough acquainted

to manage a civilized quarrel
and carried on as if nothing had been said.)

Boxers were his dog of choice
and he walked now with the latest purebred

in an unbroken line that extended
decades back to his twenties—

a mangled look about the beast, weird
walleyes protruding east and west,

massive tongue lolling flaccid
from the jaws like something dead.

When the dog punched into the trees
the bachelor turned to shuffle on,

calling for the creature now and then
with no impatience in his voice,

and I watched after him a while,
unsure what to make of the man.

His fidelity to the dumb animal.
The beating his heart must have taken.

Clearing her childhood home of cutlery
and dishware, assigning orphaned furniture

to Goodwill, dumping the suddenly
ownerless contents of cupboards and drawers

into garbage bins, I unearth a picture
from my wife's first wedding ceremony,

laid in an end-table cabinet beside
a stack of much older photographs

tracking her young parents on vacation—
a flip-book of shockingly pale skin

and pink umbrellaed drinks and hangovers
the afflicted do their best to play for laughs.

The wedding shot is solitary, the bride
standing in profile at an outdoor

table, about to sign the register
which makes the union official. A fitted

white dress, an hourglass waist, a muted
glow at the centre of marital fanfare,

clearly at sea in the public glare
of adult commitments. The groom is seated

to her left, older by a blighted decade,
already once divorced, black pen in hand

and looking something short of elated
as well—po-faced, smugly satisfied

to have survived that self-inflicted wound
and landed on his feet, one signature

shy of beginning what he imagined
would be his real life, though the donkey wager

came to no more than a repeat of past
disappointments with a much younger cast.

He was fading in the rearview before
we met, a caustic chapter she dismissed

with the barbwire humour we enlist
for harm healing beneath an ugly scar,

and seeing her beside him, on the verge
of that waste, feels somehow illicit,

a telling pre-mortem of the marriage
it would sting her even to know exists—

left hand on the spotless tablecloth
weighted by the newly-banded finger,

moments from signing away her youth
to the kind of lessons we seem fated

to learn the hard way. *Bringer of Truth*
might have served as a title if Turner

had painted those faces in another age,
one for tragedy, the other for farce.

Impossible in the moment to parse
what the chance sight will leave me with—regret

to have laid eyes on the sorry image,
or gut-rot envy for the years I lost

while she wrestled with the urge to leave,
or a shaky sort of relief that love

doubled-down when our paths finally crossed.
Or, as in most things, all of the above.

THE BETTER HALF

Ten years on, they entered the house
by separate doors and lost
one another in there. Wading waist-
deep through standing pools
of silence, a cellar's still and dank.
They frisk their pockets in an aimless
round, comb cupboards and drawers
stuffed with bric-a-brac, with junk,
as if a key has been misplaced.
Stop short when the faint pulse
of footsteps move through upstairs
rooms, when what seems a voice
eddies the quiet, a bees' nest
behind the walls, a muffled burr
catching in their clothes, their hair.

They write meandering letters
to share their days, set them out where
they might be found, by the phone,
on a pillow's cotton sleeve.
Every night they sleep alone,
startle into darkness from nightmares
that are serpentine, abyssal,
or wake to their better half
out of bed and running a bath,
the faucet sobbing across the hall.
They lie sleepless then for hours,
feeling older, more naive.
Mornings they sit in facing chairs
over coffee, missing each other.
Thinking, sooner or later
one of them will have to leave.

Lo, I stand at the door, and knock . . .
    —Revelations

They were busy at love, early on,
naked was barely enough to satisfy.
A high seriousness to their pleasures
and they undertook them as a discipline,
something to be studied and practiced,
as if they had moved into a church
and might convince Jesus to deny
the cross. When he showered, she undressed
to stand with him beneath the water's
fall, to make their nakedness ring in
that anointed ceiling's vaulted arch.

Of late, they've grown unexpectedly shy
with each other, walking through their lives
like they've never been properly kissed,
sidling up to love like teenagers
copping a feel from a homely cousin—
the body's light veiled by uncertainties,
belated modesty, their ears pressed
to either side of a door left open.
Even their nakedness reduced
to a kind of mystifying disguise.

A vintage couple, making a carnival
show of it, flaunting a parade float's
garish endowments,

mouths on them like middleweights
who are light on their feet and can
take a punch, a veiled competition

to the exchange, each the other's rival
for the camera's attention,
the invisible crowd they can sense

straining just beyond the lights.
Hard from this distance to gauge
how much of the display was real,

how much they were putting on
for a grope at shabby stardom
or a lousy hooker's wage,

though the intervening years
make it seem almost innocent,
nothing more or less than it appears,

two strangers willing to strip
and wrestle on a hotel bed
till they're breathless and spent,

a grainy seven-minute clip
of the young and immortal
before their looks began to fade

and they slipped into oblivion.
Christ, they must both be ancient
now. Or just as likely dead.

The bank job went south and the poets
are on the lam, they're sleeping in garden
sheds, they're breaking into basements
to lie low among mouldy drop sheets
and paint cans and army surplus tents.
All the money was left at the scene,
the poets haven't got two cents
to put on their eyes, they've shelled
out everything they own for a hair-shirt
and a subscription to the *TLS*.

They're watching for their faces
on the news, someone got killed
during the heist and they've heard
a rumour it was them. The poets have penned
a manifesto, they want it printed
in the papers and no one gets hurt.
They're holding themselves for ransom,
they have a laundry list of demands—
a desk, health and dental, single malt—
all they lack is a place to send it.

The poets have got themselves surrounded,
they're coming out with their hands
up. The poets are pleading no contest,
they're keeping a terminal cigarette
at the ready, a necktie as a blindfold,
they're just waiting for a firing squad
to show itself. Everything's ended
badly and they can't finger who's at fault,

whether to blame themselves or the times.
The poets have one final request
that won't be revealed till it rhymes.

Alley entrance locked, well beyond last
call, and we all but surrendered dawn
till a stranger revealed the secret sign,
knocking three times on the Plexiglas—
smoke dense as peat inside, a mirage
of pyramids beneath the billiard lights,
a handful of drinkers still at the breast.
Our waitress had the look of one chosen
to set a star-crossed world to rights
and made an effort to articulate
some riddle at the heart of ruin
before she finally drew our pints,
harping on about time and fate,
though nothing of it made any sense.
Out the window the city streets
surfaced like lost Atlantis, the bloom
gone off the year's briefest night—
perhaps I'm no farther ahead
to have spent it drunk and drunker yet,
though sober and safe asleep in bed
I'd be no further behind at best.
Tried for the name of a fiddle tune
that started up as we left for home,
but what it was, I couldn't guess.

Already several espresso coffees
into their day, manic chickadees
percolating through the backyard trees,
stitching a hangover's sackcloth from scraps
of early light with their needling racket,
mechanical snippets that ring and lapse
and ring like an army of windup toys
the night has spent all night winding.

Mindless purveyors of a joyful noise,
their sole earthly purpose is reminding
the unconscious world that morning's not
to be missed, and you won't sleep a minute
longer with the fuckers in full throat
among the birch, the pin-cushion pine,
black-capped pistons in the shining
fist of some mad scientist's machine.

Voices disembodied among the birch,
two ratchets tightening bolts
in the day's rickety scaffolding,

the crease of an old argument unfolding
in those mangled liturgical notes,
in their overlapping crank and lurch,

and a kind of scolding music to the racket,
a furtive affection in the insults
offered and countered by rote—

kiss my arse, you tick-ridden basket
of gall, you blunt-beaked phony,
you cock-sucking son of a goat,

etc—they seem content to stick it
to one another, as if company
was a whetstone meant for stropping

a broader complaint about our lives.
From where we've been eavesdropping
we see one crow materialize

in the tree's flickering crown, a blackened
branch swaying and shaking itself free
of green to improvise a getaway,

an ambling side-step, laid-back and cockeyed.
Both of us waiting for the second
to follow out of the leaves

muttering its chronic expletives,
that pot-holed voice crooked and wry,
just shy of satisfied.

LITTLE DOGS

Maldron Hotel, Cork

The hotel window looks over an ancient
cemetery where all day the city's fleet
of miniature dogs are leashed in from the street
one at a time, as if by appointment—

corgi, then terrier, then Pomeranian,
let loose to storm the defenceless green,
to strut and cock their legs and paint
the leaning stones dark with piss

while their besotted owners pace
behind and baby-talk encouragement
to the plush toys growling at unseen
threats or tearing up the innocent grass

once they've completed their piddling business.
The dead don't bother about the trespass
or the comic rigour of each pint-sized canine,
tethered long enough to this narrow plot

to have learned more than just a pocket-
dog's life looks laughable in retrospect—
our little loves, our schemes and grudges,
the mountains we compulsively construct

of nothing much before we come at last
to nothing—and seeing the truth of this
makes the departed a welcoming lot.
By nightfall, some kind soul has shut

the gate, suspending daylight's constant
traffic for a measure of the quiet
we like to think the dead are owed and want.
A church bell nips the heels of each quarter hour

but nothing stirs below or makes a sound.
Ragged cloud above, and where the sky runs clear
the docile stars step serious and silent
over that serious scrap of ground.

STARFISH

My wife is crossing the Arctic circle
when the ship goes black, three diesel turbines
kicking out, the ambient noise of fans
and fridges that wallpapered the vessel
flooding the sudden dark with absence.

Her berth is one deck below the waterline—
she hears the sea hissing across the hull
as inertia pushes the dead ship blind
against the drift of northern currents,
as she collects her headlamp, her useless phone,

her orange immersion suit. All this detail,
of course, reaches me after the fact,
when just the inbox ping of her email
undercuts the crawling time she sat
at her muster station, stress-eating raisins

and crackers with the jittery pack
who couldn't face their empty cabins
even after the engines' revival
returned them to the world of satellite
nav and radar, and she writes it as a joke,

an operational hiccup the first mate
disarmed with a radioed invite
to see the Northern Lights on the forward deck,
the company trooping outside to gawk
at the lavishly screen-savered sky.

I scroll through the half-dozen fuzzy
attachments taken on her phone (which she
admits don't do justice to the sight),
all the while picturing the splayed survival
suit where she left it beside her empty seat.

That bright starfish. Its lonely vigil.

KEEL

There was nowhere the soil gave
enough to spade a proper grave—
placed the man in a shallow cleft
above the landwash, clasped hands,
dead eyes coppered to a close.
His own boat tipped face down
where he lay, marker and coffin,
rough seal chinked tight with moss,
the gunwale skirted with stones
before we left the little craft
and its solitary passenger
on the darkest deepest ocean—
upturned keel carving a slender
passage through the seasons,
drifting each clear night across
crowded shoals of constellations.

ACKNOWLEDGEMENTS

I raised the notion of a Selected with Sarah MacLachlan at a patio bar three summers ago, when I was just drunk enough to think it was a good idea. I don't know whether alcohol had anything to do with her response, but I'm grateful to the others at our table for being witnesses to the exchange.

I tried to talk Damian Rogers out of adding "*Little Dogs* editor" to her insane list of roles and responsibilities. Thankfully, she ignored me. Dear Leader, thanks for keeping me out of the weeds on this road trip and for the echoing insight into the new work.

Thanks to the publishers and editors of the earlier collections:
Bob Hilderley @ Quarry Press.
Kitty Lewis, Gary Draper, et al @ Brick Books.
Ellen Seligman and Stan Dragland @ McClelland & Stewart.
SM and Jared Bland @ House of Anansi.

I am also grateful to the following small press lunatics:
Alan Stein @ The Church Street Press for *Viewfinder.*
GD and Charlene Jones @ Trout Lily Press for *Emergency Roadside Assistance.*
Anik See @ Fox Run Press for *Fire Down Below.*
Marnie Parsons @ Running the Goat Books & Broadsides for "Chapel Street Torque."

Thanks to the Canada Council for the Arts, without whom &cetera.

And thanks to the Writers' Trust for the unexpected phone calls.

The poems from earlier collections are printed here without changes, except for adjustments to punctuation or word choice to avoid inadvertent repetition. The one exception to this rule is "Bushed," where the adjustments kinda got out of hand. It may more properly belong with the New Poems now, but we have placed it with the other selections from *Salvage*.

Several of the new poems have previously appeared in *The Breakwater Book of Contemporary Newfoundland Poetry, Fire Down Below* (Fox Run Press chapbook), newpoetry.ca, *The New Quarterly,* and *The Walrus*.

If I had time and the mind for it, I could list a hundred people who've had their mitts on these poems in one way or another. In particular I want to thank the editors of the literary journals who have considered or published these pieces over the years.

Thanks to Holly Hogan for making me feel like I'm living a real life. And to the youngsters for making me feel like I'm earning it.

Michael Crummey is a nearly-full-time writer living something close to a real life in St. John's, NL.